# CROSSING THE RIVER

*A Book of Poetry*

BY

REBECCA LEBRON

Copyright © 2021 Crossing the River by Rebecca Lebron
Control Number ISBN:
PAPERBACK: 978-1-77419-101-9
HARDCOVER:
Ebook: 978-1-77419-102-6

All rights reserved. No part of this book may be reproduced or transmitted inany form or by any means, electronic or mechanical, including photocopying, recording, or by any information storage and retrieval system, without permission in writing from the copyright owner.

This is a work of fiction. All of the characters, names, incidents, organizations, and dialogue in this novel are either the products of the author's imagination or are used fictitiously.

Print information available on the last page.
Rev. date:
To order additional copies of this book, contact:
Maple Leaf Publishing Inc.
3rd Floor 4915 54 Street Red Deer, Alberta T4N 2G7, Canada
1-(403)-356-0255

Rebecca Lebron is the published author of Lily of the Valley Romance of Souls and went on to write this outspoken book of poetry, Crossing the River.

I was presented with Editor's Choice Award in October 2007 for Outstanding Achievement in Poetry by International Library of Poetry.

Rebecca Lebron lives in New York City and is employed as a Hospital Professional Healthcare Frontline Worker.

# Introduction

This day, I heard in your mind my first poem. I wrote it on paper and didn't stop writing.

I completed this book with a happy and thankful feeling of accomplishment.

I enjoyed writing each poem. My heart was strong and the energy from my soul shifted to my spirit which started me on a new path.

This poetry is mixed with life reality; sadness, fear, healing, etc.

Crossing the River, from one path in life to another every day experience.

May you find the same peace that I have found as you read these poems.

I have put my faith in God to enable me to accomplish what I do.

I wish to acknowledge my children who for all the years of hardship we endured, stuck together through struggle, refused to give up.

Some days we were so hungry. I would look at the fruit on the kitchen curtains and wished they could come alive.

To my friends for being there for us and helping out when no one else would,

"Thank you all!".

# What I See

I'm on my knees begging you please
come on back come on home.
I don't want to be alone.
When I look at you, what I see
is the beauty inside your soul.
The kind that makes me quiver.
A love that has with stood the
bitterness in life, the hopeless of time.
I can feel your love, a love that
we once shared when we were
young and free.

What I see is a love we had to
lock away deep into a corner
of our soul.
A love we both thought there were
very little hope of ever staying
alive. Now here we are again
in a different place and time
our aging faces and wrinkled
hands reaching out, touching each
other and still in love.
This is us, this is our love, this
is our time.

# Palm Print

My hand leave its palm print
on your face.
Every line, every track can be
Trace upon your face.

The sensation of my tender gently
Caring touch makes you blush.
Every time you feel my palm
Print on your face.

The scent of my perfume hand
Swept across your face.
As a gentle breeze blows over
My palm print upon your face.

You close your eyes, slowly inhaling
The lingering scent of my perfume from
My palm print upon your face.

Your tear gently flows
While your finger
Carefully wipe away the tear drop
From my palm print upon your face.

A touch you can't erase its
Authentic and unique because

It came only from
My palm print upon your face.

## Enchanting Room

Candles lights all over the room.
Red rose petals lay loosely
On the floor.
Champaign cooling and glasses for
two.
Soft music playing, it looks like
romance.
Sheer white curtain sway in
the summer breeze.
Moon light shines through the
window of the enchanting room.

Red rose petals float across
the room,
like a dream miracle, it brightened
up the room.
 always a hope of sweet
memories unfolding,
Which will be completed when they
walk into the room.
Each one will capture the feeling
and cherish the memories of
the enchanting room.

# Kingdom

Kingdom in heaven,
kingdom on earth,
which is the kingdom
you rather live in.
Heavenly kingdom has everlasting life.
Earthly kingdom has fortune and fame.
First think of the kingdom, then
move right in.
Which kingdom is first, you must
not rethink.

When the search begins, you
must go first.
This is no act, you can't react.
Don't compare both kingdoms
once you are in.
Live with the choices, so let
us begin.
The heavenly kingdom with
freedom and peace.
The earthly kingdom with grief
and no peace.

# What If

What if we believe this world
Is round as a circle.
If something is round then
 no corner.
So why do we say the four
Corners of the world?

What if it's an illusion?
What if deep into our souls
We believe this world is not round?
What if it is flat and has four
Sides as a square.

What if the God's of heaven who
Are guarding this world in the
Four corners
What if they stretch out their arms
And it forms a circle.

What if we're not supposed to see
The square but only the circle?
What if the shadows of the heavenly
Gods hides the four corners of the world?

What if our souls know something our
Physical mind and eyes don't know and

See?
What if really four corners of this world?

# The Heart

The heart that cries out the need
for his grace
The heart that remembers his saving
grace, will be happy in his amazing grace

The heart that desires his love
shall be joyful
The heart that are simple
many thing are made simpler
The heart that surrenders
will always remember the joy
of contentment.

The heart that are humble
the same things app
What is accomplished only in a
humble of heart
When it comes from one's heart
it's very smart.

# Disappointment

Everyone gets disappointments in
Life in someone we know sometimes
No one is perfect it doesn't exist
Disappointments exist in everyone's life

In our personality, parent-child
Relationships, love affairs and
Friendships, marriage relationship
Disappointment do exist.

Sickness and health, hope and
Sadness
Weak and strong, good and bad
Love and hate
Disappointments we do hate.

# War

War is evil, it is dangerous
War is bad the thing we hate
it's a part of life
War is the arrival of fear and hate
War is endurance chase from
a far

War is running to save our lives
War is ripping love and lives out
of our hearts
The grief we bear in our souls'
hunger, pane and fear in our eyes
war is tears and the blood
we shed

People laying, children dying
mothers and fathers lying
dead in the streets
War in the pathway, war in
the park
It is painful in our hearts

# Silent Screams

Silent scream we hear each day
Before our eyes even as we pray
Silent screams bring fear and grief
Silent screams cause sickness and death

Silent screams in the dead of the night
comes from our souls oh so quickly
Silent screams spread throughout the
world in all directions as souls
are torn away

Silent screams blends among us in
the painful thoughts of our minds
Silent screams high and low sometimes
rides on waves
Even in a bottomless pit or cave

Silent screams will eventually shine
through
So we may not lose our way
come one and all
I'll share a bit with you

*In memory of my father, who loved the sea and sat on the shore line everyday*

# Chatting waves

As I sat on the shore line
I can hear the music of the
chatting waves
Small sea crabs' crawls beside
me as I listen to the waves
Picking up a handful of sand like
an hour glass it ran through my hand

The sky, sea, land and rivers flow
where li grow
The tranquil sound of the chatting
waves put my soul at ease
The scent of the sea breeze
smell so fresh and free
It releases the mystery that
lay beneath the sea

As the waves splash against that
big old rock some splashed on
my face
The salty taste of sea water got
into my mouth
 nothing more soothing as
the chatting waves from the sea.

# Crossing the river

a river of black water
Flowing far and smooth on the
surface floats chunks of shimming
crystals everywhere you go

They are shaped as red ambrosia
only clear in color
When crossing the river if you get
into the water, it can make you
disappear

It can give you magic powers only
you can wear
River of black water will keep you
safe and free

When crossing the river say a prayer
or two
Please! don't steal from the river
It can steal a life or two
Big frozen icy cone shapes can turn
on me and you

# Our Home

When we wake up in the
morning thanking the Lord
for today in our home
Home is where the heart sometimes
finds its way back
This is our home
Home can be a mansion on the hill
An Indian teepee on the reversion
A mud hut in Africa or high in a tree
A castle hideaway or house on the shoreline
Apartment we may be ashamed or proud of
This is our home
In the depths of the getto
In the heart of the city or country side
A shack in the woods
A house boat anchored on the water
A card board box on the sidewalks
It is our home
Home is where we kick our shoes
off and take our hats off
Where we show our best and worst off
Were we cry to our hearts content
Where our family and friends gather
together
It is our home
Home is where we feel most

comfortable and safe
Where our parents welcome us after we're born
A place we smile and say goodbye
Home is our destination at the end of the day
Where we hope and pray
This is our home
Thanking the Lord for living through this day and hoping to live yet another day
Where ever it maybe, whatever it may look like
It is our home

# Only in New York

You can catch a show on Broadway
Walk on the boardwalk
Even run to cross the crosswalk
Just in time to cross the street light
You can dance in a street fare
You can march to find a cure for cancer
Run a race against Aids and Alzheimer
Or any other cause
Only in New York

Where bright lights fill the city
When hood rats come out at night
In the bright lights
House mice run against the night light
This city never sleeps at night
 garbage stinking in the daylight
Only in New York

Where people are always in a
Hurry to catch a train or bus
 always something going on
Good or bad in this city
A fashion show to see,
Sales at the malls so shop 'til you drop
Crimes on the streets and someone going down
When one learn to survive

This city some love to hate
Where everyone is welcome
Only in New York

When feet plunge through the snow
Snow shoes, map and compass
Where tall buildings grace the skyline
There are many more things to see,
Learn and discover
Where we all come together
Only in New York

Now you can decide if you want to come to New York
You can paint a picture post card scene to remember
When family and friends forsake you
When burdens are heavy
Only in New York

# Image Shadow on the Wall

Hiding behind your shadow on the wall
calling out, reaching out on the wall
Why do you hide from the evil deep
inside you?

Image shadow on the wall
Scaring others, making faces in
people places
We're not afraid of you
Fire burning, wire twisting
Teeth are shattering, cringing from
your presence

Image shadow on the wall
Bouncing like a ball, it makes
your voice bounce back at you
What are you after and what do you want?
Creepy shadow on the wall

# Hidden City of Atlantis

Your secret is safe and hidden
Searching deep and wide around
About Vanishing without a trace hidden City
of Atlantis
Ancient world of the past shifting
and moving as they pass by you
Mysterious Atlantis your secrets
Are hidden deep beneath the sea

Who's searching for the city
Wherever it may be, may never
find Atlantis
 peace and beauty in the
scenery
They're hidden from this world
legend of Atlantis
Holy Gods of Atlantis you know what
they will do

Real secrets of Atlantis you have
taken with you
It keeps the world wondering
Supernatural shield and protects
the secrets deep inside the
Hidden city of Atlantis

# Destiny

Awaits somewhere in the twilight
shadow of the horizon
The sunrise of the early morning
before the dawn tomorrow
Destiny awaits
On an island in the ocean
A rainbow in the sky for hope
 no special ingredient
One must be there in time
For destiny awaits
Open up your heart wide it will
perk you up inside
It sound kind of catchy sure
it'll make you happy
Reach and you may touch a star
Destiny awaits you
Live your dreams and remember
all the things will fall into place
There are times when things will
be rough and sometimes tough
seek and you'll find the answer
For your destiny awaits

# Bermuda Triangle

Bermuda triangle everyone wants to talk
Where did you take the people you swallowed up from
here? How did you do it?
When you swallowed all in site and
make the world wonder throughout history
Did you take them on an island out
into the Pacific Ocean or deep into
the bowels of the earth
What life are they living we all
want to know are their forces
trying to reach us from another
dimension


Bermuda triangle did you take them
on a planet deep into space
Perhaps they were sent back to
earth in different human race
Maybe as divine messengers all
over the world
Are they among us in a mist
of illusion

Bermuda triangle swirling, whirling
spinning like a world pool

You know better than to trick us
Some say it's an undercurrent
pulling everything around and in
between with dreams of adventure
In a world full of illusion, we know
sometimes things are not always
what it seems
If the triangle is not evil then it's
good with mysterious abilities
Bermuda triangle lost in a sweet
Fascination in spite of thoughts and doubts

# Deep

Deep into the earth a little
seedling covered by weeds needs
sunlight to show its beauty deep
within It must be awaken for each bulb
to flower

Deep into our hearts sometimes we
pray for miracles
Believe in miracles and you'll see them
every day in countless little ways

Deep inside us blood runs flowing
through our veins
Despite our faults he loves us
just the same
When we make mistakes in our haste
We remember his name just
the same

# Winter Boy

Shaking trying to hold back shame
Winter boy you are becoming too Cold
Wearing that same old little black
zip up hood sweater jacket
From fall to spring, no one knows your name

Winter boy
Why do you hang your head in shame
Both hands tuck into your pocket
Can someone buy him a winter jacket
Instead of him putting his hands inside his raggled jeans
back pockets

Winter boy
His face is tightened up like a jack hammer
Shoulder hunched forward as if it's
hanging on a bent wire hanger
He always walks to the back of the bus to sit in a corner

Winter boy
Everyone wonders about you
Won't it be wonderful if you
can cover up and feel much warmer

# All Together

I know you are disappointed one and all
Your tears and sadness will no longer be grief
The years of strife were part of life
Pulling together we all can enjoy life
Look around sometime we need to be alone
From this we gain the strength we need
To carry us along life path
In our hearts joy and pain
comes our way every day
Come around and have some joy

# Don't Take for Granted

The air we breathe it can
be taken away in a heartbeat
life can slip away before we
say goodbye
These things we have today
don't take for granted

Don't scorn the beggar who looks
at us today
Tomorrow we may become that beggar
Who looked at us yesterday don't
take for granted

The gift of sight
The first snowflake dancing in the air
Rain drops falling on the ground
The moon and stars high in the sky
These things we don't take
for granted

The person who in a wheel chair
a disable can't comb their hair
A blind person seeing eye dog who
stand beside the door

To make sure his blind friend
doesn't fall through the door
The chirping of the birds in spring
Which sit upon the twigs that swings
These things we don't take for granted

# Trains

Some sits on the trains all day
Riding back and forth
The conversation that go on inside the trains
You don't have to strain an ear to hear

Some speak of how hard it is to get
from train to train
The uptown trains to the down
town trains
The number one train to the number
nine trains even the A to the Z trains
So many trains it confuses your brain

It keeps you spinning all around
running underground
The subway to the railway trains
Brooklyn, Queens, Manhattan and
the Bronx, Staten Island trains
Long Island rail road and metro North too
It makes you want to go insane
when the trains all rides the same

Stand clear of the closing doors please
Standing straphangers hang on
the rails or leaning against the doors

Others grasping the hand rails
As the train rocks from side to side
Brushing up against each other side
seats are taken tightly pack on the trains

You can find every color, creed
and race stack against your face
Everyone in the same place
Steering in each other faces
How nice it is to see so many
different color faces riding the trains

# Winter Blast

There will be no classes today go
outside and play
get your sledge and ski slide
all day
Snowflakes falling down like rain
Bundle up, keep warm, don't get frost bite
Try to remember your name if the
cold get to your brains

Don't know how fast can you walk
in the snow
Until your nose and toes start freezing
your breath starts slowing
With puffs of white breath blowing,
into the wind
Winter blast how long will you last?

First shot of snow blanket the ground
looks white and fluffy as it
covered the playground
Snow stuck on bear naked trees
and those that still have leaves
with icicle hanging all over the tree
White clean snow is a beauty to behold

It sounds crisp, crisp, crisp like a

Bed of sea shells under your feet
Folks shoveling snow standing knee deep
Wet dirty snow under your feet go
slush, slush, slush it looks so messy
like a snow cone with too many colors
Dirty snow looks yucky, when it
gets all dirty the white snow
turns to gray in the height of midday
Winter blast is pounding the north east

As we go on our way then the
light of day starts to fade away
and we go inside to stay until another day
It seems like a winter blast is
heading our way every week of the month
When one winter blast in ending
the next one is starting to creep
our way
Winter wonderland when snow
comes this time
It could be the last winter
blast with lots of laughs
May be next year there might be more winter blast

# Trouble

Trouble stirs its brews like a
bitter cup of tea leaves
Stomach churns and bowels twist
A clean cup of water can get dirty
as murky water
A dash of this a splash of that add
some tea leaves
A pinch of this or that mix and taste
Making a face that spells trouble

Some more tea leaves not that leaves
Spice it up, stir and shake it up
come drink up your cup of many
tea leaves
It looks like trouble the tea leaves

If all trouble came as a cup of
tea leaves
It can be pushed aside perhaps
pour down the drain pipe
As one trouble ends another take over
It comes and goes before the
effect is over
Some people attract trouble others
trouble attract them
So, what do you do when

you're always in trouble?

Stay out of trouble that doesn't
always work
Here comes trouble walking next to you
Running from trouble it will catch
up with you
Financial trouble all kinds of trouble
Like the bitter cup of tea leaves
Make a face and find a way
out of your trouble

# Rent Drama

Land Lord calling while answering
call waiting
Wait! don't answer the tone,
another call is coming in
This might be him, don't have the
rent today
Need more time to pay the rent
this month rent

Can't pay this month's rent
How can next month rent be paid?
Rent drama begins

Notice is in the mail, you might
be evicted
Ordered to civil court be there
on time
Crowed by the dozen standing
on line
Wishing for mercy men, woman and
children
To keep their home please give
us more time while the
rent drama unfolds

# Lonely Child

Stop suffering in silent you have
always been lonely
From the age of two all alone in
a room looking at TV nine to five

Lonely child the sound of the clock go
tick, tick, tick
Foot step in the hallway hoping it
come your way
Oh no! not this way but the other
direction

Lonely child with imagery friends
Playing a game of family and
friends
Laughing and crying all at the
same time

Lonely child looking at the phone
listening for it to ring three
more times
Hello! everything is fine
when will you be coming home

Lonely child the keys are in the door
You're not lonely no more enjoy

this time now while you can
Romping and rolling, jumping and prancing
Another day is dawning

Lonely child hoping you'll be fine
until you're in college
Thanking the divine for giving
your courage, with respect and dignity

# Old Boots

This old boot has walked all
Day bearing the weight of those
who are wearing them
This old boot has worn out its sole
It was the right fit in the
right size
Walking a mile and a half

This old boot is smiling as its
past half it task
Running and playing, jumping and stomping
kicking and skipping
Stepped on hard and soft surface feet

This old boot has style
and elegance of a well-made boots
Design and plain some colors are great
How amazing they fit on the feet

# Hoops

Jumping through the hoops to get to you
From time to time, we all jump
through hoops of some kind
Even the hoops of a hula hoop
clowns jumping through hoops
hoping to oh and wow, the crowd
Who sits in a hoop looking at the view

The hoops of life we must go through
For what is the purpose of life
if we don't jump through hoop
We learn what we need to know
Armed with knowledge the universe knows

Hoops of hope and hoops of love
is the most difficult hoops of them all
We never go through
without paying a price
If we can get into the head
of the ancient one head
We'll understand the ruler of
jumping through hoops
Hoops of hope is the courage
of love
The hoops of life we must go
through

It'll grant us the wish of the
fondest wish

# Forever Young

Everything living must die
Young and beautiful grows old and
ugly
Young and tender grows old and hard
Wrinkle and aging go hand in hand
like the harmony of music that plays
in our mind
Loss of memories and gray
Hair we'll try to deny
As the hunt to stay forever young

If we could turn back the
hands of time
We wouldn't be living in this time
With lava rocks showers and lights
that zaps wrinkles
Showering our fears with high
anxiety desperately trying to hold
on to stay forever young

In time we must let go
knowing it were a waste of time
and in time everything living
must die but for now in our

hearts we'll be
forever young

# Mother Nature

Nature's fury is not something
to take lightly
It could come without a minute's
warning bringing destruction to mankind
Rupturing this earth by the minute
Earthquakes, famine, flooding
and hurricane
Can make the world grow
worn and weary
Twists and turns confuse our minds
Shattering ego of everyone who
walks on mother nature earth

Nature's bright side has spring time rain
With bright rainbows and moonlight nights
Flower garden growing happily after the rain
All of life precious things will
not remain the same
Earth changes will soon begin
Mountain peaks and valley streams

Summery breeze and autumn leaves
Will bring winters chills
High winds whistling by day and night

There are lots of memory to
cherish and treasure
On mother nature's beautiful earth

# **Rain**

Don't go out in the rain, rain
drops softly falling down the window pane
When it rains trees and flowers grows
Rainbow shows it bright glow of
colors after it rains
One can get on a train to
See the football game
Where the players play in the
light rain

Make a joke, gain a friend
come out from the rain
Don't let anyone bamboozle your
brain about the rain
Catch a plane to Port-of-Spain
Walk on plain of sugarcane
without foot pain
Some places don't get rain, too
much rain, too little rain never
again to get soaked in the rain
Please! stop complaining about the rain

# Outside Looking In

Some people go on with their lives
Not remembering others exist
Some with their face pressed
against the window pain
On the outside looking in

Crying out in shame, no one cares
about their pain
There are people who have everything
yet they complain
While others are just on the
outside looking in

Unwanted feeling fills their hearts
gleaming eyes and craving minds
Tempting thoughts with fear that
fill their heads
Reaching out with empty hands
on the outside looking in

Dreaming of what tomorrow may bring
With dreams of visions dancing in their heads
Off Miami beach and California life style

To live their dreams while on

the outside looking in

As life passes by hoping they'll
find their dreams
Some for good health and strength
Others for happiness and peace of mind
As they stand on the outside looking in

# Precious Moments

To one and all comforting feelings
Quiet moments in a garden of poems
Reflection of hope and faith
through the pathway of life
Loving treasures that's keepsake for life
Inspiration to cherish from the
tapestry of life
The seed of hope spread day
and night
Greeting from the heart is
a priceless gift
Make a wish everyday is
worth living
Seize the moment, next moment
it's gone
Morning thoughts can spill through
the night
Sunrise years will become sunset
years ending out lives
When kindness comes knocking
Thankfulness will fill the air
Precious moments we all can share

# On the Block

Sitting on the stoop, no particular
activities going on, just day by day living
Plain and simple, quite it doesn't matter
Bang, bang, bang run for your life
the police are coming
Don't look back they'll catch you
if they can
Run for cover hide in a corner
of the house
On the block
Bullet shells scatter some in the gutter
Crack on the ground look! crack
Heads are coming
Coming and going day and night
sneaking a peak across the street
Someone might get caught passing
a joint
Don't join the gangs they all wear
head bands
Holding knives in their hands
Don't start a fight if you know
you can't fight
Even if you're right they can
get you at night
On the block

# The Sun, Moon and Stars

Sunlight brighten the sky it
brings daylight
So, birds can fly all
Through the sky
The warm energy from the sun
can make us run
For a drink of water or Capri sun
Some people lay on the sand in
the sun to get a sun tan
A parade in the sun now that's
a good one, until the sunset the moon
 a full moon tonight
it looks so full and bright
Some said they have walked on the moon
Are they right or telling a lie
Sometimes the moon looks cloudy
Have anyone wonder why?
The image in the moon sometimes
looks like a man or a lady
One of the above beauties
In the sky is the moon
The stars
Stars tonight shining bright
high above in the sky
Standing proudly high and mighty

Against the blue back drop
in the sky
Captivated by the starry lights
Crowed will gather far and wide
Every night to focus on the soft bright lights
Watching to catch a shooting star
Making wishes upon that star
or something moving like a shooting star

# Earth, Wind and Fire

The earth gives us food
animals and trees too
Dust to dust ashes to ashes
it comes from the earth
Ancient city has been discovered
buried deep beneath the earth
Man were first made from the
dust of the earth
In the end we all shall
return as dust of this earth

Wind
High winds bring hurricane
blowing trees and leaves
It gives cool breeze like a
deep freeze and make one sneeze
Tornado winds twist and spins
picking up things carrying it with
the wind
The wind beneath the wings of
and eagle makes it fly high in
the sky

Fire
Fire set in the middle of a

forest, burning down the whole
forest
Plumes of fire, raging through
the air
Looks beautiful but dangerous
Run-away fire out of control
Fire raging, fire burning fire
Fire everywhere
Burning bright like, a firefly
light
Putting out fire
throughout the night
Earth, wind and fire the
elements of the world

# Sea and Land

Shimming water of the sea glitters
in the open space
Inviting for a boat race
reckless ripples with waves that
rise high
Fishes swimming sometimes leaping
through the waves
Sharks that bites, sea animals that
fight underneath the sea
Open waters of the sea sometimes
roaring, sometimes calm
Creeping in to meet the land

Land
High mountain rises high above
The land as if to touch the sky
Valley lakes and river bed, mountain
air and mountain peaks Meadowland
and camping ground Desert sand with
desert storms Forest trees with birds
nesting among the leaves
Rocky coastline with sweet
island breeze
Timeless creatures in a pond
alligator

Wildlife running and playing on the
ground
These are some of the
Beauties on the land

# Day and Night

Could it be any clear daylight
when the sun burst through the
darkness of the night
Bright orange and gold ray of light
brighten the sky and day begin
The world wakes up to a brand-new day
Everything looks clearer from the
night before
Voices are wakened then "amen"
Are said
Good morning it's a beautiful day

Night

Shape shifters of the night rattle
and roll
Male and female animals they
can become all in one
Sleeping, tossing and turning all
through the night
Restless souls hoping to see daylight
Some nights are long, some nights are
short
Weary of the long night turn on
the music and dance 'till daylight

# Past, Present and Future

Past behavior always repeats itself
In more than one way
Sometimes two or more ways perhaps
the past creeps up like a
caterpillar on a green leaf
The present
Living in the present sometimes
is hard to do
When always something
going on behind and in front of us
Keeping the present of mind the
present of time
could be wacky at times
The future
Future days what will it be like
Lessons of the past mixed with
the present
Well keep it in mind, one might
run out of time
The future is not ours unless
it is given from the heavens
above

# Heaven and Hell

Heaven is a place where good
souls go
Goes for eternity  no
weeping and moaning, groaning
and sighing
Singing with the angels at
heaven's gate
White, purple and gold are colors
that glows
Living with the angels in a
heavenly home

Hell

nobody wants to go to hell
where the devil stands with
a grin on his face
The task in hell is tiresome
it never ends
No primping and pumping on time
to waste
This strange and wacky place
is a place call hell
Where the hunt for the haunted
is always hunted in hell

# A Nobody

Some family will talk aboutyou
Make fun and step on you when you are down
They hate the breath you breathe
Laugh and talk with you as if they love you
Wishing bad thing upon you
turn their backs on you
Judgmental jumping to their own conclusion
Think of you as scum of the earth
They will rat on you talk bad about you
A nobody they will call you
Not asking a question about you
their thinking is bad about you
If they can't use you, they won't
ask your reason why
They're never in your corner
cry shame on you
So, give them something to
Talk about you
Let their words roll of your back
When they think you are a
trouble maker and a home wrecker
A nobody they will call you

# The Planets Above

Without them there will be
no birth signs like Virgo and Cancer
Taurus and Libra
To mark the sign of birthday
Wandering orbs effect sign and mankind
The powers of the planets live
above us
There would be no planetary
symbols like Venus and Neptune
Mercury and Saturn
Without these planets there'll
be no earth for us to live
No January and February, November
and December, Saturday and Sunday
No date of the year, no pulling
Power of the moon to cause tide
changes in the ocean
The sun to provide light and
heat that humanity could exist
For plants to grow and weather changes
No sun in eclipse or lunar moon,
morning star and evening star

# The Universe

Today a shift in the universe
Good or bad, light or darkness
it is full with life
First celebrate in all it
Glories Life in the waters
that flow
The wind that blows
The moon that shines
In children's laughter
Life in the birds and bees
All are in this universe
A note in a favorite song
Open your heart to hear them
Look around life
and beauty everywhere
The universe is full
when you are smiling life
is unraveling
In every season, everyday
of the year
 supernatural life
and mortal life
The universe is full with life

# The World

East, west, north and south
It jumps right out our mouth
Stand to the east to the west
the north and south
Please don't make a mess now
East meet west and creates
a mess
The eyes of the world are on the
West north and south getting out
Divided world doesn't tip on one
Side come together please work it
out Peace and love with the
heavens above
Clean up the mess pass the test
All eyes of the world are on the
west

# Dreams

A window to out soul
Dream world takes us
Home the world is in our eyes
Day dreams and night dreams
makes us whole inside

Dreams of death dreams of life
will make us sweat
It can make us wise opening
up our eyes
Even our deepest fears which
are locked inside

Astral dreams look so real
as we dream day or night
Prophetic dreams takes us
to the past, present and
future lives
The journeys our spirits take
as we sleep and dream at night
Who or what will be our
dream catcher to night

# A Single Tear Drop

Eyes well up with tears
Sorrowful hearts, frighten hearts
mournful hearts cries
All the teardrops on the world
make one giant teardrop in
a pool
A single teardrop in a pool
splash, that's cool!
Could it be teardrops missing
from the melting pot of tears
From ancient days to modern days
up above, no one knows half
way in mid air
A single teardrop fell from
the sky into a pool
splash, what a cool!

# Pain

All pain are the same
no matter where it starts
It hurts right in the heart
From the head to the toes
The elbows to the knees
It goes straight to the heart

Pain can cause shame too
If one is grinning with pain,
It hurts just the same
Calling each other hurtful names
That's pain, feeling scared and
alone is also pain

It sucks, making one rock
crying out aloud in pain
Giving birth hay it hurts
Loss of someone, love pain and
mind games
They hurt just the same through
the heart

# Freedom

Human shields on the roofs
Declared shame on you
Leader of Iraq
Sirens sounding once again
Soldiers missing from the
battle field
Dozens wounded fighting for
liberation
Open hands, hungry mouths
Tearful eyes all heads rise
towards the sky
secretly wishing in their hearts
There will be no more raging
fighting without a doubt
Hoping for peace and freedom
in Iraq

# Dance

Come on baby this one loves you
Come on dance in my shoes
Every cell in my body sings with life
Dance, dance merry music of the night
It will make you full of delight when
the sky lights up tonight
Come on dance in my shoes

Dancing shoes here we go up and
down the dancing floor
Please! don't step on my toes it'll
hurt deep in my soul
Swaying and swinging that hip in
this time
Bumping and grinning that fine oh!
Come on dance in my shoes

When the clock strikes twelve at
the time of midnight
Our dancing shoes will be out of our sight
Then we all must say good night
Enjoy the music of the night
Enjoy yourself if it's only for one night
Come on dance in my shoes

# Close Door

When a door is close
pain and fear is felt
Deep in the heart of one heart
Disappointment, shame and despair
can be seen on one face
Holding back tears with some
disgrace
Self-esteem dip to the sole of
one foot
Like a dolphin in the deep
Anxiety attack it can make
one quack when anger flash
Depression weights some down
To the dirt underground, stand
On your own grounds
Don't let it get you down be
strong
Voices of a thousand doors will
be open unto you
Get up on your feet find an
open door

# Inner Darkness

Sneaking up, creeping up
Darkness within move
away and let light in
No crawling hands slipping
under things
Tippy toe over heads
heading for the door
Inner darkness within

Everyone has an inner
darkness that lives within
Without it there wouldn't
be any human being
Good and evil, light and
darkness
The way it was meant to be
To find one's way through
the darkness that lives within

# Better Not Worse

Keep on given
Keep on living
Do what you need to do
Go where you need to be
Keep on living for what it's worth
Rise and shine live your dreams
Help him out
Help her out
Help out whoever you can
Do your thing it's time to shine
The power inside is yours
Use it the best you can
For better not worse

# The Unknown

Not knowing what you don't know
What you want to know
If you know what you don't know
Then it'll not be the unknown

If you don't know the unknown
it'll stay the unknown
But knowing the unknown may
or may not be what is good
for you
To know the unknown

The unknown that we need to
know
Will no longer be the unknown
It can change what we don't
know and what we now know
The unknown that makes the
known what it is

There are times when it is
best to leave the unknown
that is so needed to be known
alone and unknown

# Courage

If one is faced with the test
It could get stuck on you like
a hot bowl of oatmeal that sticks
to your ribs
All soldiers who had to fight you
fought not only for the people
You fought to save your own lives
That's courage
So young, so strong and brave
fighting with all of their might
Broken bones and bullet wounds
The butcher of Baghdad was no match
He hid behind the evil deep
in soul
That's courage
With all the courage of the army
You have shown him who were
with you all
Your angels stood all around
Heroes have more courage than
most of us do
That's courage
Fighting to stay alive to stay strong

Hungry for life, hungry for family

back home
Your comrades who were fighting
and those who lost their lives too
Who fought the battle for Baghdad
A city in the middle east
To free the people of that land
with true courage

This detrimental to all the United
States, British and Australian soldiers
who fought the war in Iraq
Thank you all" for your enduring courage

# Talk

Will it hurt you
To step aside, inside the train
so others may pass?

If the train is late
Will it make a difference
If you get angry or curse
Will you still get there on time?

The bus moves slow
The train moves fast
Why run to catch the train?

Want to get there fast
By bypassing the bus for the
train, it may cause you some pain
If it's not going your way

Slow down take a deep breath
walk the subway stairs
Stop the loud talking others are
thinking

# Tax and Death

Estate tax, income tax
One can't get away
from paying those taxes

The end of life we all
pay the same price
Death, no one can't run from

Not like the tax scam and
other scams
Eventually someone will figure
out those scams

If you're thinking of ways to
cheat death no way
Not this one, you can't run
from death

That's the one thing will get
us in the end
Any way it can

two things we can't
out run-in life
Tax and death

# Emotions

Emotions is feelings we
sometimes can't explain
Deep in our veins
It takes over our pain Feeling
of lost adrift run high
when emotions reach sky high

Sometimes we cry wiping
our eyes
Sometimes we laugh and smile
Other times we slip in a corner
of our self
Denying our feeling afraid
to confront our emotions

Emotions can come from
beating a drum or singing a song
Raising one's voice or waving one
hand
Silent as a lamb or roaring
like a lion
Emotions it comes from within

# Peace, Love and Harmony

Don't need to have a talent
for peace
Love leaves you with a
smile when you sleep
Harmony is one voice that
makes the same noise
When peace, love and harmony swings

Without peace there'll be
no love and harmony within
Like a fairytale story that
lives within
Unlimited feeling is guaranteed
you'll see
When peace, love and harmony swings

# Bite your Tongue

It's hanging out of your mouth
Before spitting out those words
first chew them up, swallow hard
Bite your tongue

Think, think there're people
who won't appreciate hearing
the truth
I don't mind a bit saying these
words
Bite your tongue

If always in denial never
bribe them, never award them
No judgement passing, finger
Pointing, no misinforming
Just
Bite your tongue

# When Fortune Change

One man who were to have
two wives
The first wife who should have been
were given bitter things in life
When she looked into the mirror
She didn't see the person she wanted to be
Instead the person who she were
When fortune change
The second wife became the
first wife
Who got all the wealth and
Spend it as fast as he made it
were never satisfied
When good fortune come upon some
They let others starve
As the years went by so were the
fortune
When the truth was told
When fortune change
Some stories can never change
but people can change
The first who should have been
Will eat sweet things as well
Good fortune, will be provided
in the end
The bitterness which has been given

to eat has been eaten by the one
When one story ends another begins
Both blessing of prosperity has
been to the one
When fortune change

# Slowly Dying

Some people live all their life
wondering why
The years has passed then by
Others travel far and wide
seeing many things and places
living their dreams
While others are slowly dying

When youthful years have gone
with strength and daily ability
to move
Some people count the days that
passed term by
Sharing dreams of what should have
Could have, would have been
While others are slowly dying

Some people live to be ripe old age
still doing things they love
Others lay in bed with terminal
condition
Not even remembering their name
As life goes on
While others are slowly dying
Signed living will, health care proxy

and OR     do not necessitate instructions
Emotionally and mentally fami
tries to except the pain of what
will be
As they watch helplessly their
love one's
Slowly dying

# The Eyes of Faith

Though the eyes of faith
our mind can heal
From the doubt life may bring
use each day
It may teach us how to make
better choices everyday
Take a leap of faith it'll get
you there
The eyes of faith
Sees beyond today only
We can choose the way
It can change things around
in a better way
Faith can make us listen to
our heart
Making us see and think clearly
like the light of day
Through the eyes of faith

# Wonderful Day

Have a wonderful day in
every way
Laugh and play have fun
all day
We're here today don't
stand in others way
Go see a play, call someone
today
Take some time off, help someone
Have a wonderful day
Read a book anyone you chose
Be amused when you wiggle
your toes
Don't pick your nose,
While you starting to dose
It looks so gross that thing
hanging from your nose
Go do your thing but not anything
Have a wonderful day

# Berries

Berry, berry blueberries, strawberries
and cherries too
Grape with raspberries and
cranberries
All of those are good for you
Bake with them, eat them to
Drink some of these berry juice
Fresh and sweet delicious to
Here! taste some of these
Colorful fruits
Wonder what it'll do for you
Strawberries and raspberries
Cranberries and blueberries, grapes
and cherries
All of these six berries
Che-rasp-blu-gra-cran-stwis good for you

# Intuition

Is a gift from heaven
It's a feeling deep inside
Sailing from the inside out
All the answers we'll ever want
lives just a few doors down

Intuition tells us when something
is wrong
Even stops us when we are
taking a wrong turn in life
It's the nagging feeling that
will not stop

Intuition, don't worry if it hurts
It can make you laugh cry or scared
It always tells the truth
That feeling we sometimes ignore
You'll never know if you don't listen
to your intuition

# Share

Share knowledge and wisdom
don't take it with you
Share a space with someone
who may like you
Share a meal or two it's not
all about you
Share the clothes on you back
don't ask for them back
Share the car you drive if a
friend needs a ride
Share prayers when you pray if
someone is listening
Share a dime if you can not
because it shines
Share a smile when you're
walking a mile
Share the music in your
heart that's the way it all starts

# Want-to-Be

Hey! my mother, sisters and brothers
call me a want-to-be
If my father was alive I bet
he would call me a want-to-be
How about you calling me one too
Maybe I deserved that to
Someday I'll be a somebody and
not a want-to-be
With all these talents God has
given to me
I know somebody out
there
Who don't want me to be a
nobody want-to-be

# Mother and Daughter

I'm the first born of your ten children
I'm not your favorite or never will be
Nothing I did was good enough for you
I was never the apple of your eyes
You chose the others my brother and sisters
We fuss and fight sometimes all the time
My brothers and sisters were always
in your sight
You cheered them on, helping them
to be strong
You put me down, I always knew
since I was five you didn't like me
mom
I have done something's wrong when life
got me down
You told my children when they were
very young
That I was as cold as ice
A child you never trusted a wicked child
Who will be alone in this world
You told my daughter she'll be like me too

Oh! Mama dear how could you
be so dam dear mean
You hated our father as much as you

hate's me
I was the one who always
Protected you
I stood in the middle when you
were fighting
Afraid he would hurt you
I never hated you, I just didn't
like you
If wasn't for you I wouldn't be
born
One of your daughters said I
should be dead
You second the motion
One day her wish will come true
I'll be dead
Oh! sister dear one day you to
will be dead we all will be
dead
Thank you mother for giving
me life
I do hope you have good dreams
at night

# Strength

Some people get carried away
with strength
Like Samson and Delilah
Strength is believing in one self-
admitting when you're wrong
Standing and not running when
things don't go your way
Strength is facing it head on
whatever it may be
Standing for what one believes in
even if other may think you're wrong
Strength is challenge to protect
oneself and others from harm
Strength is courage, strength is
honesty
Strength is only when the strong
survives

# Balance

In life and death
The minute someone dies, someone
else take's that place in life
Your life, my life every ones life
The balance between life and death

Your breath, my breath
will become someone else's breath
You don't like I don't like
Love and hate, short and tall
The just and the unjust, lost and found
The balance in life

Heaven and hell, light and darkness
good and evil
Night and day, laughter and
tears
Up and down, up above and
down below Land and sea, river and stream
All of these are the balance in the world

# Don't

Don't do this or that
Don't go here or there
Don't touch this or that
Don't eat from the dish
Don't taste that It's bad for you
Don't wear that outfit can you
see it don't fit
Don't mess with me you're a pest
Don't you know that word is a curse
Don't drive my car you may go
to far
Don't lose the shopping list you
better be listening
Don't go down those stairs you
might be in tears
Don't care about you, water and
oil just don't mix
Don't plant the rose bush close
to the edge
Don't is a word we all use
each day
Don't touch that dial

# In the Box

Living in the box so dark and cold
Can't touch my soul, can't reach my goal
Peaking through a hole, oh God make
someone please touch my soul
In the box
Suffocating my own soul can't breathe
underneath all this dirt
Bouncing my head from sun up to
sundown
Wondering when am I going to reach
my goal
In the box
One foot hanging out of the box
Seven days a week Lord I
feel so weak, walking this mean street
My head is spinning looking
for a way out
In the box
I want to eat, live, sleep, breathe
and relax
Like a sheep in the meadow
So free and tame
I want to keep it real to live
My dreams and taste victory
I'm stepping out of this box

# <u>Alright</u>

There're eyes looking down
upon us
With open hands and fingers
touching our souls
Everybody who have a need
Everything will be alright

Always open, always loving
When times are hard and pain
is all around
He'll be there to comfort us
with open hands
Everything will be alright

Like a star we can shine
in his eyes
He don't mind who we're or
what we're
He'll be there to hold our
hands anytime night or day
Everything will be alright

# When Love Fades

Like a feather that floats away
in thin air
Chasing, running, reaching to touch
Something one we can no longer have
Who would be here to heal us
When love fades
Disappearing out of reach empty
feeling
No joyful feeling when every
thing is question
Broken hearts  nothing
else like
When love fades
A little bit of this a little bit of pain
So much tears it feels like
rain
feeling can't explain when
things aren't the same
When love fades

# Struggling

Struggling to make ends meet
can't eat or sleep
Take a peek, can't keep things neat
Walking up and down the streets
into next week
Can't pay the bills trying to
climb the hill
Winter, spring, summer and fall
It's a long, long road with very
little clothing
Working nine to five it's not a
Cat's life
Luxury is just a dream if it
can't be real
Struggling to make ends meet

# Underneath the Tree

Falling leaves will hide your face
You'll lose yourself, fool if you
think your safe
Don't stand, don't sit, run as fast
as you can
From underneath the tree

Tump, tump take a chance face
the world
Step out into the sun
Don't stay in the shade it'll make
you afraid
Run as fast as you can
From underneath the tree


Dance, dance for a while fancy
foot step
Prance, prance think of how you
used to be
Now with sunshine in your eyes
Don't be afraid to lose control
come out
From underneath the tree
Stomp, stomp don't be crazy don't

do it alone
Swing and run dance and prance

Take someone hand run as fast
as you can
From underneath the tree

# Turning Around

Sooner or later taking your time
Make up your mind if you
want to stay where you are
If you don't want it
Turning around

Yes or no, go or stay, here or there
Deep in your heart the strength
is within
Sooner or later the wheel
will be
Turning around

Don't say everything is fine
Searching far and wide high and low
Wondering if your heart has found it's wings before
Turning around

If you let it be the way it
should be
Your wings will fly straight across the sky
Shooting like an arrow from cupids bow it'll be
Turning around, turning around

# Running

Running for your life
Running all alone when nobody cares
Running from someone
What do you do when you're
running from the invisible ones
Where do you hide when you're
running from your home
run, run, run

What do you do when you're
running from yourself
Running down the stairs
Running in the streets
Stopping to breathe, looking all around
Everybody is always running from something

# Get Ready

It's a long road to travel
Stepping over gravel
Shubs on the side, water in
the drains
Kicking up dust leaving a
long trail
Get ready

To go on a journey around
the corner
Where no movie stars
Standing on the corner
Only street venders selling their
stuff
One for a dollar two or more
Just regular people making a living
Get ready
To go down to the sea shore
Where there're footsteps left
behind
Soon they'll be fading in the
sand
One by one as they disappear
from our mind

# Are you Listening?

To the music on the radio
and the stereo
It's coming from the CD like
a free-b
Classic R&B you better get
ready to rock steady
Hip hop makes you hop that's hot
So you better shut up
Blue grass that's in its own class
Country music that's good music

Are you listening?
To the voices in the wind like
the windmill
That's easy listening when nothing
is missing
It keeps you guessing so don't
be missing
When the artist are rapping
They're telling their stories
to fame and fortune
That's good listening
Are you listening

# Sound

Everyone has a sound in their
heart
The sound of a baby cry, children's
laughter
In a special place in their heart
A sound of a boy or girl a
woman or a man
In the back of their mind
Sound of their mother or father
brother or sister voices
They always will remember
The sound of a happy or sad song
repeating on their mind
Sound is everywhere moving fast
Please pass that glass, go to class
Hear the sound of everyone's
pain it almost the same
Sound

# Just Don't Fit

You told me you were out with
a friend
Who had lend you a helping
hand
Then you were out roaming
the land
With one of your lying friends
That just don't fit
You told me you were out last night
You thought you might turn around
and run
When you were having a drink
with someone
That just don't fit
What are you trying to say
We can't no longer be friends
Did you find another friend was
it your plan all along
You said no you were sick
That just don't fit
I saw you holding her hand
When you drove through my neighborhood
You left me all alone waiting for you
to come
When you were having fun

That just don't fit
I've seen you with my own eyes
When you saw me in the corner of
your eyes
You drove as fast as you can still
holding her hand
You said that wasn't you
That just don't fit
You better get out of my face
You're a dirty lying man
I don't have to put up with this
Please get out of here don't
say you're sorry
That just don't fit
I'm telling you it's over now
You said that was just an old
friend
What am I supposed to believe
When you're lying
Right to my face, I can't trust
your words
I don't have to put up with you
This one just fit

# Searching

You been running around over
town
With your tongue hanging out of
your mouth
Like a dog you're in this whole
dam town
Searching
Like vinegar and wine, you
dine them
Until you were out of a dime
As a hot summer's night
All the time they dazzle
your senses
Like a stroll in the forest
Searching
Finally, you're starting
To settle down
Its crystal clears the town
words echoes in your ears
Calming and soothing your mind
Sweet, fresh and zesty will
help ease you
Searching

# Say Goodbye

I feel it in my heart
I feel it in my soul, in my gut
In my mind I feel it just the same
It's time to say good-bye

It was swell and it was well
Even if no one could tell
I have to leave even if it's
in a rush
It's time to say good-bye

My eyes are weary it's also teary
My feet are uneasy it's getting ready
I don't want to sound to needy
Seconds count they add to months
It's time to say good-bye

 a craving feeling in my
stomach
It's not for packing food or
burning calories
It's for moving on, carrying on and
not waiting for the dawn to come
To say good-bye

# Fifty Years

Fifty years is not old age
It's golden years and many years to have lived
In all the years one has lived
Fifty years is a lot of years and one to wish
Who have lived for fifty years
Know the wonder years should be the best years
Half a century and not yet laid to rest in the cemetery
Fifty years and hoping to live for many more years
From one year old to fifty years old
Looking back at our life track we have passed
Our bodies may sag and some maybe glad
About the different changes and
imperfections in our faces
Our minds may drift, our eye lids
may need a lift
Our eye sight may have lost some of it
glow
Our hair may be thinning while
turning gray

We grew bloom and open, like
a flower with it's radiant beauty
Which everyone have admired for it's beauty
Is wilting slowly now that we have turned fifty

# Thank You

For the friendship you have found in us
The help you have given to us
Standing with us when things go
wrong
Even when we're right or wrong you
never frown
Thank you
You gave and gave, we took and took
You never said no even when you
know we'll come back for more
When others have shot their doors
in our faces
You open up your door not even with
an ooh!
Thank you
When others have turn their back
on us
You open up your arms and took us under
your wings
You sang to us hymns and they
gave us the grin
You gave us food when we're
hungry as the eye of a storm
Thank you
You have comforted our hearts

When we had nowhere to turn
From dust to dawn you've protected
us from falling down
You've pulled us through the cracks
When our back were stuck against
the walls
Thank you
So kind, so giving with a heart
and soul
Fill with kindness enough to share
with many more souls
You'll not be the forgotten friends as
others have done
For everything you have done for us
You know there will be many
more thank you to come

# Souls

Find the goodness in your soul
Then transfuse it to your heart
Let it flow into the world
If you have a very old soul
You must know what is your goal
From your very old soul
Find the mole, keep your eyes on the goal
It may sound old, low and behold
Don't sell your own soul or anyone's soul
Not for this world it'll end up in a hole
With mournful groan the fright from one's soul
That very old soul will roll in the hole
will it float or sail when it leaves
this world
Who will pay the price
When that very old soul
reenters the world

# Beware

Beware when the tides come rolling in
when the gray clouds cover the
sky
When sons and daughters leave
their parents home
In search of their own dreams
Some may find it some may not
Some may forget who paved their
way to their success
When success comes to their hands
They may park others next to the
night stand

Beware of the promises and plans
they might make
On their way to success street
When getting there it may be all
grins and smiles
Wait a while some may make their
parents cry
Never lifting a hand to help the
old man
Never caring if she can still work
With her hands the old lady who
may need a helping hand

# Fear

Fear is gut wrenching, heart
pumping over time stomach crunching
Fear is head spinning out of control
neck aching, blood pressure rising
Fear is eyes popping out of it's socket
teeth shattering, tongue tied, dry mouth
Fear is finger snapping, body shivering
feet are shaking, palms sweating
Fear is dying over and over while
still breathing and alive
Standing, sitting walking or
running
Fear even makes us afraid to
sweat, it makes us afraid to sleep
Fear makes us afraid to fear

# Wheel

This wheel begins at the top and
ends at the top
Round and round it went on and on
Nobody knew how it would end
nobody cared
Months went by into years, many
Years
The wheel kept spinning on and on
Into the core stored goodness for
a lifetime
Round and round merry go round happy
was the song
Evil claws snatched at the wheel
pulling out the core
Robbing it from the goodness it
once stored
Now it's time to close the empty
circle on the door
Buried the hatchet lock the door
finished the chapter
Close the book that looked so good
The inside stories is full of horrors
It goes deep into hell
The wheel life has ended the
chain is still bounded

Memories burns deep like a whole in
the ground
Where the wheel began it end once
and for all
The wheel of life always has stories
that burns to tell, to all of it's friends

# Riding the Fences

Riding the fences between
light and darkness
Between God and the unGodly
good and evil
Riding the fences between
right and wrong
The wings of love, power and greed
beneath the stage
Riding the fences between
right and wrong
The wings of love, power and greed
Which is the need, find a place
beneath the stage
Riding the fences between here and there
Still feel the greed, still hunted by the need
Riding the fences between life
and death forget them not
Read the lines between the life
chart before taking the path
When riding the fences between
God and the unGodly
Between light and darkness, good and
evil, right and wrong
Power and greed, here and there
Life and death

# Collecting Thoughts

Short and sweet it looks so neat
Need some sleep go count sheep's
Go through the tunnel that looks
like a funnel
Run with a windmill to the top
of the hill
Pop some corn girl don't scorn that one
Get out of the vice don't throw
that dice
Stand back and kick it up a notch
A good attitude on one will intrude
Take a nap, then snap at that quack
What's on the inside will eventually show
on the outside
Experience is wisdom no one is stupid
Silence will eat at one nipping silently deep
from the inside
Don't feel ashamed if you're called
nasty name
Deal with the pain it'll not make
you feel vain
Hate is blinding to the human eyes
and mind it grows like moss
It seeks revenge in wicked
Destructive ways

# Pushing

At work, school or play
Someone is always pushing
Standing on line, on the train,
on the bus, at a sale someone
will keep pushing, pushing

At a party on the block
A fight on the streets
Bet your life someone will
start pushing, pushing

One day someone will push to far
They may push someone right out
of their mind
Out of a job, out of a home
Someone will keep pushing, pushing

On the sly with  age
race and work discrimination
 When one no longer can serve their
purpose
Someone will still keep pushing, pushing

# Listen Up

Listen up, please don't stop
You can make it to the top
If you should stumble on a block
Don't look back keep on looking
at the clock

Listen up please make up
Don't act as if you are shock
From your gut feeling the luck
It'll get you at the top
Believe in your stuff

Listen up please don't get drunk
You'll smell stink as a skunk
While on line please don't dine
Someone wants to get to the
front of the line

# Free our Souls

Free our soul let it fly like
a kite high in the sky
Where airplanes fly's day and
night high in the atmosphere
Fear only what's coming from
our soul, we're not without
sins
Free our souls
Weep and pray let our soul
rise high above
Like a dove it'll fly away someday
and may return here to stay
In a better way God will help
it along the way
Free our souls
Not only for today he'll light
up the way
With his angels on both sides
lending a helping hand to the
grand stand
let us free out souls he is
here to stay

# Away from Home

Today I heard your name and it
sounded just the same
Lord! how many miles are we
Away from home

Well today we hope and pray
that you may help us in many ways
Father, son and holy ghost
Away from home

In this world of today there're
many dangers along the way
Lord! you're on, you're two, you're three
all in one
Away from home

So much pain, we take your nam
in vain
Some even go in sane
Others die for your name, while
Away from home

# Sound Asleep

Sound asleep, unconscious to
this world
No now or later, not even a
creature
Could have awaken you, no existence
as if we were never born, as we
lay sound asleep

No human form, no one to scorn
No signal, no sound no knocking
We can't think whether we
live or die
It's so real, it's not a big deal
After all it's just a big dream
The show goes on every time we're
Sound asleep

It makes one think how did you
not hear
What went on out there
A crime happened it could have been
to you
Someone needed help with hope and
faith
Who were full of fear, you didn't

hear, you had no fear, you were
Sound asleep

Outside your window, outside your
front door
Someone tried to brake open
your home
They tried to jimmy your lock on
your front door
How did you not hear what went
on outside your front door because
you were
Sound asleep

# Mean People

So mean as sin, can't get a
true grin out of them
The act of the devil will not
take them to heaven
Mean old man standing on his land
Grabbing from the hands of his
tenants
Chasing them out for one or
two months rent

Mean people trying to scare
their tenants out on the street
Putting crazy glue all up into the
key hole
One by one night after night
Buying the hands of idle young men

To scare his tenants out of their minds
Mean people put them to stand
All in one line, one by one
Let them stretch out their hands
all day in the sun
See how long they can stand the
heat of the sun
They'll beg for shelter, just like

The poor tenants
When their mean old ways flash
In their minds

# Heart and Soul

Our heart keeps us alive
Our heart makes us feel love
and pain
Our heart can be transplanted
replacing another heart

Heart and soul
Our heart is for this world
Our soul takes us to the after
world the after life
Eternal life will be our best life

Heart and soul
Our soul may return to
fulfil another goal
Compassion in our heart, faith in
our soul
The trademark of our life,
Deep in our heart and soul

# Black Out in the City

When the lights went out in
New York City, summer 2003
Hot and sweaty we were not
neat and pretty
Some packed like sardines trapped
in the subway
So dark and smelly, tired hungry
sleepy and weary
Let's stay together until the
Light are back on
Do you believe  no light in
New York City

Black out in the city, history have
been made again
Young and old, rich and poor
Thinking about home when will
we get there
Thinking about their love ones
Some sleeping on the dirty ground
No matter where they came from
 a heat wave in the city
All over town, when will the light
be back on

Black out in the city
Scrambling for, water, candles, flash
lights, radio and batteries
No red lights, green lights, no
spectacular lights tonight
No dancing tells the twilight
We were all praying for daylight
Buses in the city were all giving free rides
Until the light came back on
Just in time to brighten up the night

# Believe it or Not

Thunder and lightning it sound
very frightening
Hurricane and storm warning
Stop yearning
Strong winds and sand kicking
up on land
Water keeps poring over
Flowing where the young ones
play Heavy rain bringing down
terrenes
Houses floating by with precious
memories inside them
Their owners saying bye, bye
with tears in their eyes
Waving goodbye without raising
their hands
Big fallen trees lay dead on the
ground as water keep lapping against
them
Green and dried leaves blowing in
the wind
No one cares about them
Mud slide slipping downhill
It's all against their will
Boats sailing in the streets
one might think they are sailing

on a stream
Everyone needs answers we
have to let it be
It's greater than anyone, it's
words of wisdom
Natural disasters, any disaster
makes our hearts and minds
grow stronger, it moves us
Believe it or not

# Against all Odds

always a way out you
just have to find it
We all had to find it
All the worrying, the uneasy turmoil
All the budding was not a destination
putting all that stuff behind

Against all odds
Sometimes it was too
much
Pain and suffering, tears and
sorrows
Hopping for a better tomorrow
If there was a short cut
That road would be real hot

Against all odds
Don't leave it to chance
When the wind is whipping the waters
your chance to find
·a solution
It takes a little effort
You have made it; we have made it
Others will make it too
Against all odds

# New Song in your Heart

Put a new song in your heart
When you start to lose your
own song
When heaviness is weighing you down
The enemies will take pride
in keeping you down
Prove to you, take the
wand in your hand
Waving it around, no thoughtless
thinking
Find strength and courage, find a
new song in your heart
Keep a good attitude take the
chance
Rise up march on, sitting down
can make you forget your song
Encourage yourself, tune up your
senses
All the darkness in the world
can't put out the light
In your heart if you don't
let it
Your wishes and dreams are precious
When you forget your old song
Put a new song in your heart

# Joy

Think about the good things the good times
in life
When things were going right
Moments of kindness, compassion
and peace
Joy and happiness is simple
pleasure
Playfulness, humor and love, caring
and sharing
Food, flowers and wine
Joy of giving back when the magic
is flowing in our soul
No holding back not even from
the mask
For what's inside our heart is
a field of love
Promises some we never kept
and forgotten dreams
With joy and emotions everywhere,
everyone can walk on to a joyful
song

# A Flower

Grows, bloom fad wither and dies away
If you're afraid of dying you should not be
What you hear coming from the inside
Is your frighten heart beating
Because you know we're here
for a little while

When the light of day is fading
the darkness falls
When the night is finally over
then comes the dawn
Live life like a flower beautiful and sweet
Spreading our fragrance far and wide
Don't be afraid when it begins
to wither and slowly fading away

When the day that our flesh
are weary and slowly dying
If we lived just like a flower
 nothing to be afraid of
We too could be happy
Fading away making room for
others
To grow and bloom just
like a flower

# Divided

Parents and children some may
be divided
Brothers and sisters, sisters and
sisters
Brothers and brothers, sons against
daughters, daughters against daughter
Sons against sons
Sometimes we can't explain
Divided by nature or divided
by greed

If the heavenly father had two
sons the first and the second son
If the first son, he thought would
be the good prince
Became the greedy prince and
were thrown out of heaven
cursed and bewildered as the
prince of darkness
The evil one, rebelled against his father
Divided by nature or divided
by greed

The second son the gentle soul
the anointed one

The good prince, the prince of
light
He fills the world and light
Up a smile
He showed some the way, who
followed his ways
Miracles he performed, he healed
the sick, he raised the dead
The prince of light and the prince
of darkness
Divided by nature or divided
by greed

Parents and children, sons and
daughters, brothers and sisters
Scholars and teachers
This is a question, in this poem
Who were the parents of the prince
of darkness the evil one
Did the heavenly father have two
sons who were like Cain and Abel
Divided by nature or divided by
greed?

# Eyes

See others through the eyes of
our soul
Not the eyes of the devil, the eyes of hate
The eyes of lust and greed

See others through the eyes of
a child
The eyes of the very old through
their heart and soul
Not the eyes of looks and the
eyes of wealth

See others through the eyes
of grace
Not the eyes of fear, when they
are in despair
The eyes of vengeance or the eyes
of death

See others through the eyes of love
Not the eyes of another
Take time to heal the pain
Take time to see others
Through the eyes of your own
eyes in life

# **Divine Intervention**

You were there, you answered
our prayers
Near and dear you share your
divine healing

You anointed our bodies when
we were laid up in bed
You patted us on our shoulders
whispering in our ears

Words you knew we would hear
So near and dear you sheltered us
When we were full of fear
You strengthen our faith

Night and day we mourn and
groan full of pains
No one was there to hear
our prayer

You sat with us and kept watch
over us
Divine intervention we'll always
remember

Far into the future how you never
forsaken us
The heavenly angels who came in
our dreams and vision
To heal our bodies, to soothe our
hearts and souls

# See No Evil

We know evil exist
we all try to resist
The axes of evil that comes from
the devil
The bowels of hell pulled out from
the devil
Wicked and smelly, no one can tell
What dwells in his belly
gushy and nasty
That sin we call evil

Hear no evil
Only if we're deaf in our minds
As time passes by it run through our mind
The evil sound of a wicked mind
Cursed hands that rob many
their lives
The sound of evil everywhere
we go
Like grains of sand, it
Blows throughout the land
Sound of evil which comes only
from the devil
It lives in our world that is
Its goal

# Breath of Life

She said they were coming
closer
One by one here they come
Three of them one in front
of her
One on the left and one on
the right
She can feel their present
the angels of death
Their present are strong, it's
not her time yet
They stop calling her name, her
life is speared
How frightened she looked, that
look on her face
This night she couldn't speak
But her eyes spoke just the same
mommy please do something quick
to ease the pain
In my chest it's pressing my breath
before my breath stop with tears
on my face
Help came in with a small cylinder of oxygen
A fresh breath of air, a breath of life

# You Pick Me Up

You pick me up when I had fallen
face on the ground
You dust me off and send me on my way
You stood by me, you let me lean on you
You wipe my tears when my eyes were full
You were my truth when I couldn't
and didn't see the truth
You were my eyes and made me
look towards the sky
You were my strength when I was
weak and weary
You free my soul from its tormented life
Who else would deny me a
right to live
You gave me bread and I was
able to raise my head
You took my hand; you lead me
from the cold
Just in time, you helped me save my soul
You made sure I didn't change
my mind
You were the bridge I stood
on in the midst of the storm
I didn't run because you made
me strong

# The Edge of Time

Standing on the edge of time
it may have slipped our mind
The ray of sunlight, the rain falling
on the land
It's all standing on the edge of time

Depending on what direction the
wind blows
The whistling, howling, mournful, creeping
melody the wind makes
Can cover the earth when the
wind blows
Which is standing on the edge of time

Remember while the earth remains
Life will not always be the same
Celebrates the good life the
good times
Together we're standing on the
edge of time

# Pit of their Hearts

In the pit of their heart's feelings
sunk as deep as a shopping cart
The flame in their hearts burns
like wild fire
Through fear and loneliness, rejection
and scorn
Like a rose with torn and horses
running through the storm
They never gave up trying to be
strong
In the pit of their heart
They had enough down fall for
twelve life times
It's the signs of time and they
don't mind
Perhaps they both listen to their
hearts
To the words that was already there
and they were not aware of They
have everything their hearts
desires
In the pit of their hearts

# Across the Sky

Someone said if we had
wings, we'll fly straight
across the sky flying high like
a kite
Miles and miles with a smile we'll fly
Some of us like a bird, like a
plane, like a fire fly
Across the sky day and
night, we'll fly
Feeling the wind, feeling the breeze
beneath our wings
Strong and weak, sun and rain
Across the sky fast and slow
we'll fly
Hot and cold someone says free
and wild
Up above down below. flapping our
wings like a butterfly
Across the sky sun up to sun
down we'll fly
Like a child's glowing eye don't
know why
Joy and pain what's to gain
It's a shame we don't have
wings to fly
Across the sky

# The Other Side of Life

In death who wants to bet
without breaking out in a sweat
From here to there, the journey between
life and death
One is afraid to share the thoughts
when we think of death
What is waiting for us on
the other side of life
Shall we think of heaven and hell
with a smile
The smell for hell is so rotten
and full of scorn, everyone settle a score
Heaven smell is wonderful you don't
have to yearn
Why be torn between heaven and hell
The other side of life
No day and night, no fighting to
be right
Heaven dawn, one lives long
crowned by happiness
Hell, lives in turmoil
fill with hate  no date
When we think of death that's
a lot of sweat

# Standing Beside You

I stand beside you, only with you
In this moment that touches our heart
This is our moment in time
 no mountain high enough
or desert sand you haven't crossed
to be here with me
If I had your way, I had to lose
you, never wants you, never love you
You have destroyed the trust
because of pride
Once again in this lifetime
The we have loved each other for
ancient of years and still won't let go
That's the way it is you and me
forever and always
Our last chance, God knows we
should get it right this time
Two hearts two soul bounded and
chained together for all eternity
Somehow found their way back
into this world
Here I'm yet again still
standing beside you

# One by One

See them run some all at once
running for their lives
This is real, it is reality as it
unfolds
They have no goal, the gold they
wear can't take them anywhere

One by one begging for a dime
under the bright shining sun
Some kneel and pray to live through
another day
Some pray to take them away they
can't stay everything is taken away.

One by one trying to pick up the
pieces
Piles by pile searching for love one
underneath debris
Someone helps us please; we can't take
any more
We can't find no peace, where's peace

# Sitting on the Sidewalk

See that old woman who's sitting
flat on her butt
Walking cane lay close by her side
No one knows where she came from
who gave a dam
How did she get there or ever care
Sitting on the sidewalk
Her legs out stretched, covered up
with old lining cloth
No one knows what is under the cloth
Sometime watching her drag
shoppers walk by some stepping
over her
Not one excuse me please, I'm sorry
mam, watching her
Sitting on the sidewalk
Dark eyes piecing, gazing at every
one, her voice very low
How can anyone go without giving
her a dime
Please help me, she cry can you
spare me a dime
We have seen many people like
her everywhere we go
Sitting on the side walk

Who have let themselves go, dirty
and stinky, hungry and needy
Some of us turn our heads looking
the other way
Hurrying away forgetting the person
Who looks like a side show just
Sitting on the sidewalk

# Can't Speak

They stood watching the children
play
It seemed they knew not what to say
They stopped, then I said are you
joining the others
They looked straight ahead without
saying a word
Then I knew they couldn't speak
My God please forgive me for
whining all the time
You gave me ears that I can hear
all the time
Feet to walk to take me places
I need to go
Eyes to see the rivers that flows
Mouth to speak, to laugh and to
sing
My God please forgive me
Sometimes I do not think
Instead I whine all the time
I'm blessed with all my senses working
fine
Blessed those who can't hear
Bless those who can't see
Bless those who can't speak

# Once Upon a Time

We loved to dine in a little cafe
overlooking the river bay
Moon light flicking on the water
Music playing in the back ground
Over and over again penetrating
The hearts and souls of the young
one's

Once upon a time
Everyone felt pretty there were
No wailing words of self-pity
As the caravan of love, everyone's
were happy
Now it doesn't seem so faraway
Remembering the weariness that
even woos sleep

Once upon a time Life was simpler too
No wishing wells or casting spells
The young ones, the lucky ones. the
free and the wild ones
Some steal away into the night for
a ticket to paradise

Once upon a time

Browse in now and then, hour and
for years
Searching for the inner most being
Drawing of wisdom from a fuller
richer happier life
Now times has change and we have
changed

Once upon a time
Fairy tales were told now real
life took its path
Where skipping stones and rocks
and stones lay peaceful in the
water still
So much for feeling safe and worry
free
Life is full of ups and downs

# The Man without a Soul

Open your eyes into your heart
Open your heart let it flow into
your mind
Whatever you do or say may
follow you someday
When the wind blows, you'll know

You live in mourning night and
day
how can you ever find your way
You roam where wild horses will
not run
You have learned how to cry
Be not discouraged, be not disparate
Look inside yourself you'll find
your soul

# Wired Up

When a pin drop, we stop, to
See who got pop
Some cop shot him until he dropped
Some dam con, stole some coins with
Some dollars at a bank
The talk of an accidental, hit and run
A gun went off and someone got shot
we're wired up
Sweet kids at school some wearing
invisible mask
People are wired on drugs, anorexia
bulimia and weight loss
Diseases, illness, hunger and crimes
nightmares and worries
We all need, more courage, more
money more, more of everything
We're wired up
On something even on the internet
and network TV
Shopping at the malls and super market
even star crazy
Plastic surgery pulling tucking and nipping
Movie's goers looking for the best movies
Wired on wars lying, stealing and cheating
Everything that goes on in life
We're so wired up

# Eye of my Soul

So big and bright it shines from the sky
Like a storm of fire raging through the night
One soul maybe two or three each one has
a different goal
It is not cold as ice, it can pierce through
the heart
Slicing it like a piece of pie
It is very old, older than this world
One eye so many souls
Roaming this world like a magnet it
can pull truth and
Funny as a clown, magical and powerful
exciting and fascinating
Young, old even the unknown soul has
its aims and goals
When it enters into the world
Through the soul  a whole
new world
Destined to penetrate the heart and
Soul of who believes in the eye of my soul

# Our Heart Frets

Beyond our troubles, our pain and
our worries
Rocking back and forth again and again
It won't get us anywhere without
more pain
Fighting, struggling, ruthlessness and
cruelty survival of the strong
Our hearts frets
confusion, despair, dishonesty
and failure
Getting to the threshold our heart
may sink in fear
Some of us maybe weakened by
worry and stress
Breaking down under the pressure
of life
Our heart frets
God has given opportunities
unlimited to mankind
Yet we fumble around miserable
and bitter
From the four corner of the
World all ages race color or
creed
Our heart frets

# It's Human Nature

Why do we do the things we do
treacherous against each other
When we're full of sorrow it's difficult
to find comfort
Only by learning how others behaved
in their own sorrow
We can lessen our pain
All the sorrows and pain in the
world couldn't sink anyone soul
Until we let it get inside our mind

It's human nature
To condemn, to run away from the
hurting
Midlife crises, drama in our lives
Selfish and self-centered tearing each
other down
It is important for us to want to be
Happy
There're people all around us who need
our words to build them up
To nurture, to show courage, to share
to encourage them
Take time to share a gentle word

# Three Pennies

Three pennies are all we have
Holding them close to my heart
First one represents the father
The second the son
Third penny the holy spirit
holding them as tight as I can
Some may think it's not enough
When you trust in the heavenly
father, He'll multiply them one by one
He'll always meet our need

All we have is three pennies
Holding them in my hand
A cloudy day, a heavy heart He'll
turn our day full of sunshine our
heart full of happiness
With lots of smile
We've trusted him and believed
in him
As I hold my three pennies tightly in my
hand

# As

As high as a mountain
As rough as sand paper
As free as a bird
As beautiful as a flower
As smooth as butter and gently
as a lamb
As passionate, cruel and painful as
love can be
As worrisome, anxious, nervous and
frightful as a time line
As soft as a cloud
As a puff of breath on a cold
winter's day
As there are many more words
we can say
As playful as a puppy
As beautiful as the sunset going
down
As someday we all will be gone

# Hope

Hope will raise you to the level
you want to be
The more you say it the more
it'll come to past
Use your words to bless and
make your future
Hope is an open, mind, heart to heart
You're what you're inside you
Let it shine
Be a dreamer, dream out loud
Look to the heaven, look to the
sky

Don't be afraid to hope and pray
Hope day after day listen to your
own words
Little by little it'll begin to happen
It'll rock your heart and pierce
your soul
Make it happen be true to yourself

# One Chance to get it Right

If you had one chance to get it
right
How would you do it and what would
you do different?
Would you scream, would you have
a fit
Wishing you were in the middle of
nowhere
That you're a victim in your life
Roaming like an alley cat
Would you cry out loud jaw dropping
heart stopping
Tears cascading down your face like
a waterfall?
Say tomorrow is another day
What if it could be the one last
breath
What would you do with your
One last chance to get it right?

# Thankful

I'm thankful for breathing
that means I'm still alive
I'm thankful for saying my prayers
that means I can speak aloud
I'm thankful for the sunrise
that means I can see
I'm thankful for the loud noise
The garbage truck makes early in the
morning, sometimes it makes me mad but
that means I can hear
I'm thankful for smelling the roses
that means I have a sense of smell
I'm thankful for doing all my
physical duties
that means I'm healthy
I'm thankful for this day
that means I can enjoy it
I'm thankful for eating my meals
that means I can thank God for
everything in my life
I'm thankful for a place to rest
my head at night
that means I have a shelter over
my head
In everything gave thanks

www.ingramcontent.com/pod-product-compliance
Lightning Source LLC
Chambersburg PA
CBHW070100120526
**44589CB00033B/1171**